Compete

Gain the Winning Edge in Sales with the Attitude of Elite Athletes

Michael Sadeghpour

Compete

Printed by:
CreateSpace Independent
Publishing Platform

Copyright © 2017, Michael Sadeghpour

Published in the United States of America

Book ID: 150901-00228

ISBN-13: 978-1545438589
ISBN-10: 1545438587

No parts of this publication may be reproduced without correct attribution to the author of this book.

Table of Contents

**Can a Shift in Mindset *Really*
Increase Sales Performance?** 1

**Three Ingredients to
a Winning Mindset** 5

**Confidence - Not All Thoughts
are Created Equal** 8

**Talking to Yourself - the
Inner Voice that Drive Us** 14

**Six Steps to Building
Sales Confidence** 23

**Let's Talk Job Security - the
Real Elephant in the Room** 26

**Feeling Overwhelmed?
Inevitable or Manageable** 33

Final Thoughts 38

Can a Shift in Mindset *Really* Increase Sales Performance?

Let's cut to the chase: traditional sales training is incomplete. I say this because the mental side of performance—and yes, sales is a performance-driven business—has never been an integral component of sales training. Over the years, sales organizations have worked diligently to arm their sales forces with what I would call traditional sales training—the strategy and tactics of how to become a trusted advisor to current and future clients. What does "traditional sales training" really mean? Simply stated, it's the mechanics of selling: territory development, account planning, targeting your audiences, prospecting, conducting high value conversations, pipeline management, understanding your product, negotiation, closing, and so on.

Of course, this training is helpful and necessary. But my 30+ years of being in the business of sales has taught me that it really is not enough, not by a long shot. We are missing a critical component to sales performance, and we are doing our sales organizations a major disservice by ignoring the mental side of sales. Given the competitive landscape that exists for all businesses today, we need to examine what skills will equip our salespeople and sales leaders for success in this environment.

Here are a few sobering statistics from leading firms that track Business to Business (B2B) sales:

- 74% of B2B buyers conduct more than half of their research online before talking to a salesperson (Forrester Research).
- 5.4 people are now involved in the average B2B buying decision (Corporate Executive Board).
- 75% of B2B buyers now use social media to research vendors (IDC).
- 90% of decision-makers say they never respond to cold outreach (Harvard Business Review).
- 74% of buyers choose the sales rep that was first to add value and insight (Corporate Visions).

In today's technological landscape, salespeople are up against a more complex challenge than ever. Salespeople and sales managers are under constant pressure to hit numbers, and when that pressure feels insurmountable, pessimism takes over. When optimism disappears and pessimism reigns, confidence drops. When confidence is low, we allow negative and destructive thoughts to occupy our minds, undermining performance. When confidence is high, we have thoughts that are advantageous. Sales is a mental game.

Psychology, we are realizing, is an integral component to modern sales. Consistent success in sales cannot be achieved without mental toughness, or "having your mind on your side more often than not," as defined by Dr. Jim Loehr, a leading sport psychologist and co-author of *The Making of the Corporate Athlete*. The reality of the modern buyer highlights requirements of the mental and emotional makeup needed to be a top performer. Where else do we see top performers? On the playing field.

More than any other business discipline, sales professionals are like athletes. Their performance is measured in terms of wins and losses, their accomplishments expressed in hard numbers by the week, month, quarter, and year. Athletes are defined by passing yards, runs batted in, goals and assists, and the like. But unlike athletes, where intangibles like attitude and confidence are known to dramatically influence performance, salespeople are trained and managed like workers on an assembly line. Companies dedicate time and resources to sales training, skill development, and technology while neglecting to investigate the mental and emotional components of sales. Sales is a performance-based business, and yet important factors to a successful performance—like attitude and perspective—are being overlooked. Salespeople have the mechanics down, but just like in sports, there is more to success than just the mechanics. Traditional sales training is incomplete.

We have an opportunity to tap into the mental training elite athletes leverage to perform at their best. Yes, there is in fact a strong comparison to be made between successful sales professionals and elite athletes, which by definition of their name—elite—are also consistently performing with success.

Three Ingredients to a Winning Mindset

Elite athletes work to stay in a "winning mindset." Ask yourself: is your mindset working for you or against you? The winning mindset combines passion with intent; it sets the tone every day towards your stated goals. The most successful elite athletes know these three ingredients:

1. Attitude. Think of attitude as an energy source. It is the fuel that drives your motivation. Your attitude forms your mindset, which controls your emotions. Your emotions dictate your behavior. Individual contributor attitudes, both positive and negative, will affect team performance and morale. Remember: emotions are contagious. Others will learn from you. Positive people produce, negative people consume. In many of my workshops, I ask attendees a simple question. When you don't have a positive attitude, how does that affect you at work? At home? The consistent themes are as follows: motivation decreases, quality of work suffers, productivity goes down, and attention to detail diminishes. At home, you often are in conflict with your family and strain relationships, you act irritated, you feel lethargic. We all

know what this mood does to the amount of energy and focus in your personal tank.

2. Effort. "Just enough" is not enough. Effort is the byproduct of your attitude. Most people put in only what they believe to be the required level of effort, and this is reflected in performance. Top performers, however, regularly exceed requirements. They acknowledge that their performance will wax and wane over time, but use a positive attitude to drive consistent high effort levels. When I begin coaching sessions, people tend to ask, "how long is this gonna take?" I can't answer that question. The answer depends on how willing you are to put in the effort to get what you want. In fact, I could be asking you: how long is this gonna take? Without enough fuel in your tank, it will be a challenge to reach your goals.
3. Ownership. Are you half-in or half-out? Or better yet, all in? Ownership involves self-direction, self-motivation: an intrinsic desire to improve. It exists in an excuse-free environment where individuals commit to mastering the fundamentals without being directed to do so. Without a sense of ownership, excuses and diversions rear their ugly heads. I commonly hear excuses that shift the blame: the market's not healthy, the

product doesn't work, our demo of the technology is insufficient, customers are impossible. While there may be some truth to these statements, you ultimately make the decision not to let these excuses own you. You can prioritize and put the effort forth needed to achieve your desired outcome and own it. Elite athletes understand this component better than most because the desire to find a competitive edge has no time limit. It is not based on external forces, rather, it is based on being willing and committed to achieving your desired goals.

So, is your mindset working for you, or against you? Alright, let's get to work.

Confidence - Not All Thoughts are Created Equal

Your fleeting thoughts are more influential than you think. Revered sports psychologist Dr. Bob Rotella describes confidence as "an aggregate of thoughts you have about yourself." Confidence is an ever-changing state of mind due to the power of these thoughts. Your confidence level is based on the ratio of positive to negative thoughts: more positive thoughts than negative will net a high confidence level, more negative thoughts than positive will net a low confidence level. All of your thoughts contribute to your overall confidence level, but some thoughts are more powerful than others. Recent thoughts can influence your confidence levels more than thoughts that occurred in the past, and thoughts you connect with strong emotions are typically more memorable, meaning that they can be more influential than thoughts to which you have attached little or no emotion. One recent personal failure can destroy confidence built up by weeks of small victories. One major breakthrough can boost confidence that was consistently low. Not all thoughts are created equal.

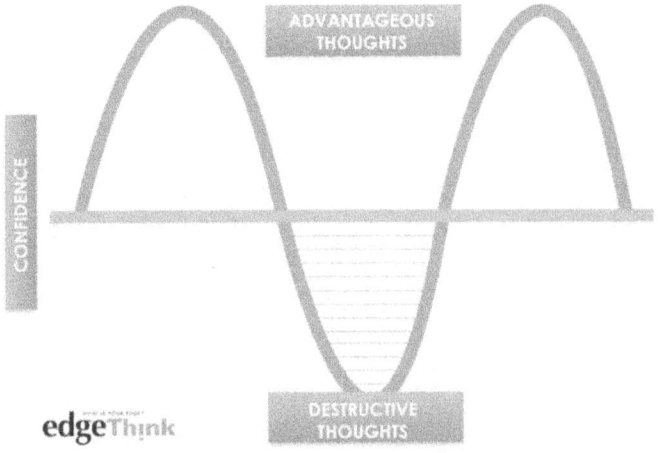

Confidence goes up and down. I like to visualize confidence on a graph, like the one above, where wavering confidence soars above and dips below a threshold. When confidence is high, above this line, thoughts are advantageous. During coaching, when I ask salespeople about the thoughts they have when confidence is high, I get similar answers every time. *I'm feeling great, can't wait for my next call, can't wait for the next team meeting, maybe I'll get that promotion after all.* When confidence is low, below the line, people report having destructive thoughts. *I'm doing poorly all around, I don't want to make that next phone call fearing it will be another setback, I'm afraid I might get let go or fired.* Confidence will always, to some degree, go up and down cyclically, but you can train yourself to have high confidence levels more often than not.

Elite athletes know that the key to confidence lies in practice, repetition and adjusting based on feedback. Feeling prepared and fit fuels belief in future success. An elite athlete begins with self-assessment (as you will do in the quiz at the end of this chapter). They survey all aspects of performance, identify their weaker areas, and go deep with it. Then, they practice. They practice on their own, they practice with a coach, they practice with teammates. They collect all the available feedback, make adjustments, and from there, they perform. But even if they haven't improved as much as they'd hoped, an elite athlete does not allow a negative event to drag down future events. An elite athlete is trained to compartmentalize, or how not to think of setbacks as indicators of future performance. In baseball, for example, a hitter has multiple chances at bat. Let's say the hitter goes up in the first inning and strikes out. It is critical that the hitter compartmentalize this setback and detach it from upcoming at bats. He can take lessons from the strike out, such as a certain pitch that he saw, or certain movements by the catcher to predict the pitch, but that's all. He can't go up thinking *I struck out the first time, I'll only strike out again*. Instead, he has to think *Sure, I struck out the first time, but here is a new opportunity to focus on the task at hand and execute*. A salesperson can think in the same way after a sales call that didn't go so well. Think *We'll set up another call. We didn't lose the deal, we just didn't close it today* rather than *That was a terrible call. They'll never do business with us after that.* This is destructive thinking. No matter how true it feels in the moment, do not connect negative events with future events.

As a professional salesperson, losing a big opportunity to meet or beat your quota is a very powerful emotion. And if not handled correctly, it can eat away at your confidence, and over time undermine your self-belief, resulting in a pattern of destructive self-talk. The key here is to get specific by methodically breaking down your performance. There are five distinct skills to build the blueprint for a great sales performance. The first is **product** or **service knowledge**. How well do you understand what you're selling? A good salesperson is able to effectively communicate the benefits of his or her product, talk about the competition, and make a case for what his or her product does better. The second skill is **situational knowledge**. This is how well you know your audience. This, for example, is your understanding of what a chief marketing officer is looking for, and how they measure their business differently than a chief technology officer would. They have two different viewpoints, two different sets of priorities, different metrics, and different criteria for buying products and services. The third skill is knowing what company sales tools are available, or the **company capabilities**. How effectively can you use company tools to reinforce your value proposition to your target audience? Whether it's a white paper, a reference story from another client, or an ROI calculator, you company offers valuable tools to assist you in making that sale. Take advantage of these! The fourth skill is having a **solid sales methodology** or **sales process**. Have a procedure in place to get someone into your sales funnel, learn what they are trying to accomplish from a business perspective, what the buying process will be on their part, how they make decisions and measure investments, and understand where you are in that buying cycle. This will help you to figure out what your next steps should be, and help you forecast your business and sales. The fifth and final fundamental skill is **managing your own attitude**. How well do you handle setbacks? Can you learn from them?

One way to effectively pull yourself back after a loss is to reduce the negative mental chatter in your environment. Negative mental chatter becomes overwhelming when you're too worried about what other people think, panicking over what happens if your plan doesn't work out, when it all becomes too much. Defeating the stress of mental chatter can feel like a battle raging within your mind. But there are steps to reducing the chatter. The chatter can be external, it can be your ringing phone and the people around you, the social media that's ever-present in the background, or the busywork you use to distract yourself from the real task at hand. Chatter can also be internal, it can be the mental gymnastics you put yourself through, projecting worst-case-scenario ideas of things you can't control, magnifying the negative, and jumping to conclusions. Overcoming this is the ultimate challenge to us as emotional beings.

Talking to Yourself - the Inner Voice that Drive Us

Our "inner voice" shapes our emotions. Our emotional state impacts the quality of our focus, pace of learning, and ultimately, our performance. Our "inner voice" is the manner in which we explain life's events to ourselves. Raising our "inner voice" is the first step to unlocking the keys to effectively navigating our emotions. Elite athletes work with sport psychologists to learn from losses and setbacks, and incorporate those lessons into the next performance to be successful in the long run. The better we understand our own psychology and emotional tendencies, the better we can bounce back from negative events. This will affect your confidence levels and how consistently you perform. Creating and maintaining confidence is not only based on our emotional state, it is also very dependent on our mastery of skills needed to compete at our best.

Evaluate your abilities in each of the areas (laid out in the assessment below) and see where you can improve:

Self-Assessment: Confidence

Instructions:
Answer 4 questions for each topic, scoring on a scale of 1-5.

    1=None
    2=Below Average
    3=Average
    4=Above Average
    5=Excellent

Once you've completed the quiz, you'll be given your total coaching assessment score (100 points possible), as well as individual scores for each area of sales competencies.

By assessing sales competencies in each individual area, you will able to quickly identify strengths and pinpoint the areas where improvement is needed. Strengthening these skills will help you build confidence!

Product Knowledge:

How well do you understand the products/ services you are chartered to sell? How well do you articulate what the product/ service does to drive business metrics? What is your ability to answer top-level questions in order to be credible with your audience?

Score	Capability
	You feel confident describing your value proposition to your target audience.
	You can effectively position products and/or services in opposition to your competition.
	Your ability to connect business impact to your products and/or services.
	You are comfortable answering specific questions about your products and/or services.
	Total

1=None 2=Below Average 3=Average 4=Above Average 5=Excellent

Situational Knowledge:

The ability to establish credibility with your target buyer(s) by understanding their top initiatives and the market issues driving investments and resource allocation. This can also be defined as the environment to which you are selling (CMO, CTO, CSO, CFO, etc.) as well as the focus of the executive and his/her team.

Score	Capability
	You are knowledgeable with your target buyer(s) business language. (For example, A Chief Marketing Officer and his/her team use the following terms when reviewing key business metrics, "Cost of New Customer Acquisition", "RFM (recency, frequency & monetary value) of existing customers", and "Life Time Value".)
	Your knowledge of the key issues and challenges facing your target audience (where they invest their resources).
	You are able to establish credibility with your target audience.
	You are confident in understanding the buying processes, or "internal sign-offs" of your target audience.
	Total

1=None 2=Below Average 3=Average 4=Above Average
5=Excellent

Company Capabilities:

Your ability to leverage sales tools created by your company that reinforce your value proposition to potential buyers. For example: case studies, white papers, ROI calculator.

Score	Capability
	You can effectively leverage company-created sales tools, reinforcing your value proposition to the target audience.
	You can effectively position company created sales tools versus your competition.
	You can competently connect company sales tools with the target audience's business issues and key metrics.
	You are able to incorporate content experts within your organization (when appropriate) to enhance value proposition and advance the sales process.
	Total

1=None 2=Below Average 3=Average 4=Above Average
5=Excellent

Selling Methodology:

The chosen process implemented across the sales organization to manage opportunities and base forecasting. You can quickly identify where you are in the sales cycle. You are able to take specific actions to move the sale to next step in the process.

Score	Capability
	You are knowledgeable of your company's chosen sales process.
	You understand where you are in the sales cycle.
	You are clear on the number of opportunities needed to meet or exceed your quota.
	You are able to forecast your business accurately.
	Total

1=None 2=Below Average 3=Average 4=Above Average 5=Excellent

Attitude:

You approach every day with a plan of action to meet your goals. Your mindset improves performance. When you have setbacks, you are able to compartmentalize and learn from them, instead of allowing them to derail you from your goals. You have the tools to change the lens through which you view the inevitable pressure that comes with a job in sales. You understand how to use cognitive skills to create and maintain a positive mindset to perform at your best.

Score	Capability
	You handle setbacks quickly and effectively.
	You are able to reset and refocus when things are not going well.
	You are able to handle pressure by preparing and practicing effectively.
	You believe in your ability to be successful and that your behavior has a direct impact on your success.
	Total

1=None 2=Below Average 3=Average 4=Above Average 5=Excellent

Score Guidelines:

Add the numbers in each section to create a total overall score of your confidence in your sales fundamentals.

My Overall Score is _____ of 100 points.

	Assessment Result
Product Knowledge:	Scored _____ out of 20
Situational Knowledge:	Scored _____ out of 20
Company Capabilities:	Scored _____ out of 20
Selling Methodology:	Scored _____ out of 20
Attitude:	Scored _____ out of 20
Total:	Scored _____ out of 100

90 to 100 points: Very confident
80 to 89 points: Confident
70 to 79 points: Average confidence
60 to 69 points: Below average confidence
0 to 59 points: Low confidence

Your Score Breakdown

The key to understanding and interpreting your overall score is how each sales category contributes to your sales competency. By evaluating each sales skill, you are able to focus on the area(s) that require improvement. Check any categories which received 15 points or fewer:

Score	Category
	Product Knowledge
	Situational Knowledge
	Company Capabilities
	Selling Methodology
	Attitude

Six Steps to Building Sales Confidence

1. Assess Capabilities. In order to understand your strengths and weaknesses, it is critical to objectively assess and establish your baseline of sales competencies.
2. Prioritize Areas of Focus, Based on Assessment. Focusing in one specific area is the most effective way to make positive progress.
3. Practice with a Purpose. Prior to practicing a particular skill, ask yourself: "why am I doing this?" Connecting effort with desired outcomes is a very powerful motivator.
4. Visualize Success. Through your own eyes, see yourself successfully executing a particular sales fundamental during a sales engagement.
5. Perform. It's game time! Go for it, this is the moment for which you have prepared.
6. Critique Performance. This is the most important step. Whether you do it yourself or solicit feedback from a peer and/or manager, the goal is to purse excellence, not perfection.

Utilize these six steps and you'll have what elite athletes have: a blueprint. This blueprint is a plan that allowed athletes to maintain their confidence levels as they perfect the fundamentals of their sport. A blueprint in sales will help you leverage these skills into a stellar performance. You'll solidify a mastery of skills, and this is one of the elements of creating your competitive edge. You have to consciously decide to create and commit to your blueprint. Elite athletes make a choice to find ways to get better. They embody what's known as the "growth mindset."

Dr. Carol Dweck of Stanford University has conducted extensive research on achievement and success. In her book Mindset, she goes into debt defining and illustrating two types of mindsets through her research. She contrasts people who display "fixed mindsets" with those who display "growth mindsets." People with fixed mindsets are risk-averse, failure-avoiders, meaning they connect ego with mastery of their particular discipline. Fixed mindset folks are not likely to put themselves out there.

People with the "growth mindset" focus on their love for learning, which drowns out the fear of failure. Looking at every situation as a learning opportunity—and yes, you can learn from failures—trains your brain to break that fixed mindset and create a habit of optimism. People who adopt Dweck's growth mindset, including elite athletes and top sales performers, are constantly striving to improve.

They leverage their winning mindsets, optimistic attitudes, and emotions to create a competitive edge. To apply sports psychology to sales and take on the mindset of an elite athlete, ask yourself: how do I get better? How can I consistently improve?

Remember the three pillars of a winning mentality. Your attitude influences your effort, which affects your sense of ownership. Believing that you can improve will fuel you to get to the next level. Improving isn't about being perfect or never making a mistake, it's about the pursuit of excellence and embracing a growth mindset.

Let's Talk Job Security - the Real Elephant in the Room

There's one thing in sales that everybody knows but might not be willing to admit: it's all about job security. It's the elephant in the room, it is omnipresent in the mind of anyone carrying a bag for a living. So right now, you're probably thinking *I understand and agree with some if not all of what has been covered so far. However, how do I shift my thinking away from "job security," and balance the demands of making my number and redirect to a growth mindset? If I don't make my number, even if I'm showing improvement, I'm out.* Ok. I hear you, but does this type of thinking galvanize development and sustainable long term performance? The path to improvement can feel messy and hopeless if we do not identify and embrace the barriers preventing us from continuous growth. Let's take a step back and break the "job security" fears into digestible components

Here are the influencers that impact our belief in one's ability to be successful. The threat of "job security" allows these influencers to trigger a survival like instinct and behavior because we connect them to potential failure. The perceived totality of these influencers can project negative emotions, creating a sense of doom. Our interpretation of these influencers shapes our emotions and our emotions drive our behavior.

edgeThink

The first influencer is **your quota**, or the set goal of what you have to reach in terms of sales for the company. Your quota, and whether you meet it, is how management views your productivity. The second influencer is **your pipeline**, which is reflective of all the opportunities you're working on. Your pipeline should provide you with enough leads to attain your quota. The third is **your forecast**, or what you need to achieve on a weekly/monthly/quarterly basis to your manager. The forecast is directly correlated to your pipeline, which is fine-tuned to help you meet your quota. The fourth influencer is **your W2**, a term in the sales world for how much money you'll make at the end of the year, as reported on your W2 tax form. The W2 is what you've actually produced at the end of it all, and hopefully exceeds your quota.

Even for the best salespeople, at times this can be overwhelming the key to turning these influencers into a roadmap to growth is stay focused on your inputs versus outputs by influencer. For example, your forecast is not strong enough to make your quota. There are two influencers which, if not managed properly, will put you in a negative mindset because you are connecting a weak pipeline to quota attainment (and job security) versus identifying specific inputs to grow your pipeline over defined period of time. Grow your pipeline by 50% over the next 90 days in order to forecast at or above your quota. Identify specific actions with timelines and measurements (inputs) that will drive pipeline growth. Easy enough right? Wrong! The tendency is to focus on the end result of 50% pipeline growth and not on the step by step tasks aligned to pipeline growth. Attitude, effort, and ownership must be fully aligned in order to achieve 50% pipeline growth in 90 days. People tend to fall into two categories when faced with this challenge: they see it as a threat, or as an opportunity. If it's a threat, you act defensively and seek excuses as to why you shouldn't or can't commit to fully to your goal. You play (sell) on your heels, and the fear of making mistakes and/or failing leads to underperforming. When salespeople are in a defensive posture, they tend not to ask probing high-value questions that might challenge the prospective buyer. They shy away from difficult objectives and slowly begin to give up. As a result, the conversation that they're having or actions they are focusing on are not of high-value, but minimal (if any) value, because they are not approaching the opportunity with a plan in mind to move the conversation or challenges forward.

This reaction is known as "threat rigidity" and narrows what you view as your options, and undermines your ability to stay focused on the present instead of worrying about the outcome. Imagine having this posture while trying to process information and think on your feet, which is essential to sales success. It would be a difficult journey. In contrast, if salespeople approach this same situation as an opportunity, the conversation and the questions are typically more thoughtful and of higher value to the buyer. With a positive mindset, salespeople aren't afraid of pushing the buyer to think differently or explore other options. If you adopt the winning mentality of elite athletes and see sales as an opportunity, you set goals for yourself, play on your toes, and your approach is to exceed expectations. You want to exceed your numbers, you want to make as much money as you can. Your positive or negative attitude, seeing sales as an opportunity or a threat, dictates how you behave. Your outcomes are directly influenced by how you look at what's ahead of you. Here, the mind leads the body.

Remember the three pillars of a winning mentality? Attitude, Effort, Ownership. These translate well to the sales world. And the parallels between sports psychology and sales psychology do not stop here. Elite athletes choose to fully commit to continuous improvement in the pursuit of excellence; not perfection. What does this mean? It means that not only do they believe in their abilities, but they also believe that with the right focus, they can improve those abilities. Think about motivation: what is more motivating to the human spirit than the belief you can reach new heights in your chosen field? The pressure to excel can be a positive influence, if viewed through an opportunistic lens. Some stress is good stress. Pressure can be a motivator, given that you have the right perspective. Your perspective gives rise to your "inner voice," which dictates your reactions and responses to a situation. For example, the pressure of public speaking can lead to positive or negative thinking. When viewed as an opportunity, we more often than not are able to harness our nerves and emotions to work for us, not against us. When viewed as a threat, we have cognitive and somatic negative reactions. Racing heart, heavy breathing, excess perspiration. Similar reactions occur in sports.

Professional golfers, for example, know how to cut through the noise and focus on the task at hand. Player A and Player B are both on the 18th fairway of a major tournament, with significant money and a five-year exemption to keep their PGA Tour card at stake. They are both 150 yards from the green with the opportunity to make par to win the tournament. Player A asks his caddy, "How far to the pin?" His caddy tells him, and advises he use a 9-iron. Player A takes the club and starts thinking about outcomes. *If I make par, I'll win this tournament. $1.4 million, private education for the kids, pay off the mortgage, get my wife a nicer car, and keep my Tour card for five years. Hold on, how* *far to the pin again? This is a 9-iron, right? Okay, okay. Focus. I hope I hit a great shot.*

Player B has the same conversation with his caddy. 150 yards, a 9-iron. Player B takes the club and goes through his pre-shot routine. He sets his sights on the flag, perfects his angle and alignment, takes one practice swing, and goes for the real thing.

Which player is going to execute more often than not under pressure? Player B, because he is focused on the execution of the task, not worrying about the outcome. Take this situation over to the sales floor. Salespeople without the psychological training are more likely to focus on outcomes, and completely forget about the task at hand. Exceeding quota would mean a hefty bonus, which would mean a nice family vacation and new bicycles for the kids. Well, that hefty bonus is not going to be awarded if you don't focus and hit your quota in the first place. In the moment, salespeople, who aren't adequately prepped for this moment, crumble under pressure. Elite athletes train their whole careers for that game- or tournament-winning moment.
They break the insurmountable pressure down into specific actions.

Adapting the mindset of an elite athlete, fusing the winning mentality with the technical skills of sales training, will create a competitive advantage in sales.

To compete at the elite level, salespeople and sales leaders must integrate the mechanics of selling their particular product or service with the ability to harness emotions and consistently perform at their best. The key here is to think like an elite athlete. What would a top sports player do when faced with a challenge? To succeed in athletics, as in sales, you have to break down overwhelming circumstances into specific, manageable areas. Strategically create goals you can meet and actions you can control. Set goals that include actions which align with meeting or exceeding your prescribed quota. Take steps to build yourself a pipeline that can support your quota goals. Achieving each goal helps you keep up with your forecast, which maximizes your W2. Breaking down a challenge into specific steps shows you what you can control. When you identify what you can control, you can adjust your outlook, and succeed in the pursuit of excellence.

Feeling Overwhelmed? Inevitable or Manageable

Think about how you feel and how you act when you're overwhelmed. Imagine: you just got your quota and it feels too high to be achievable. You're looking at your blank spreadsheet and frantically trying to figure out how to hit your numbers. The stress from this uncertainty triggers an emotional and somatic response, which leads you to feel like you're heading in ten different directions at once. If getting from Point A to Point B were represented by a line, it would look like this:

This scenario is certainly less than ideal. Too much energy is expended in the process of getting from A to B, and the reward (total sales) is low. A top athlete would approach this situation by slowing down, and creating a set of concrete, achievable actions to work towards the goal.

Pausing to take control helps, and even cutting down your stress—and therefore your superfluous actions—by fifty percent will clear your head, lower physical stress responses, and potentially double your bottom line

This is better, but it's possible to cut stress even further. Some stress can be useful; it can jumpstart your motivation and inspire you to perform well. It's when stress builds too much, when the line between A and B spirals out of control, that stress becomes detrimental to your sales goals. Getting a handle on things by slowing down your mind and prioritizing realistic steps will exponentially increase your bottom line.

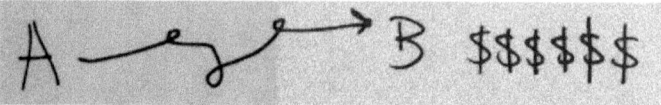

To successfully break down overwhelming circumstances into manageable tasks, apply three filters to the situation. First, what are the facts? Separating the actual facts of a situation from your interpretations helps you apply your second filter: what can I control? Or, perhaps more importantly, what can I not control? If you know something is out of your control, trying to gain control of it is a waste of time an energy. This time and energy could be better spent elsewhere, in pursuit of some other goal.

This time and energy could be better spent somewhere you know you can make sales, make money, and increase your W2.

The third filter you apply is your own perspective. The way you interpret your surroundings determines how you react, because your perspective dictates your emotions. On an average day, a human being will have nearly 65,000 thoughts. Without a good filter, something to tell us what is true and what we're just imagining, this is enough to overwhelm anyone. A good perspective acts like a mesh sifter when panning for gold, or like a colander when draining water from pasta, to let go of the negative thoughts and hold on to the positive ones. Over time, this filter will train your brain to interpret events with optimism, which will help you build the confidence to succeed in sales.

This three-step process is what Dr. Martin Seligman of the University of Pennsylvania calls "learning to argue with yourself." It's a productive form of self-reflection that forces you to slow down, put pen to paper, and organize your task into manageable steps. To perform like a top salesperson or elite athlete, learn to recognize when your emotions are getting out of control and train yourself to slow down and readjust your filter.

Let me use a personal example to show you how to readjust your filter. Not long ago, I suffered a heart attack while at home with my family. In the back of the ambulance with the EMTs from my local fire station, I followed my own advice.

I first asked myself, what are the facts? Here's what I came up with:

- The echocardiogram shows my heart is in distress
- I am having a heart episode, according to the EMTs attending to me
- The EMTs are experts and well-trained to administer short-term care to people in my health state
- I am in the best hands possible and on my way to a team of experts waiting for me in the ER

Here's what I could control:
- I can cooperate with the EMTs and do what I'm told
- I can ask questions in order to gain as much clarity as possible on my medical situation
- I can answer their questions honestly and accurately

Here's what I could not control:
- My diagnosis and the severity of my condition
- What hospital I will be going to—each, as you know, have their perceived pluses and minuses
- Medication going into my body and the types of potential surgeries I may be facing

This was my perspective on the situation, based on looking at the facts and figuring out what was under my control:
- I have had a heart attack
- The advancements in medicine have enabled people like me to recover to a healthy life style
- I am an active 52-year-old and as a result, I am positioned well for a strong recovery

I realized the situation I was in, and harnessed the power of positive psychology and Seligman's technique of arguing with myself to find calmness during this time. As you can imagine, I had every opportunity to allow my mind to take me to some pretty negative places. If this technique worked for me during a health crisis, it can work for you on your next sales call.

Final Thoughts

The next frontier in sales performance is training sales professionals in the proven techniques of performance psychology. I feel privileged to coach sales professionals at all levels, as well as amateur athletes, on finding their specific blueprints to growth and achievement. Without question, the relationship between sustainable high performance and a growth mindset are consistently at the forefront of what I see as a high-performance coach. Dr Edward Hallowell in his book titled "Delivered from Distraction" describes our emotions as the on and off switch to learning and engagement. If we are not learning and growing as sales professionals and athletes we will miss an opportunity to gain a competitive edge. Thank you for investing your time in this book. Here are five tips I hope you take away to help your continued pursuit of excellence:

1. Remove the noise. Zero in on what will impact your desired results instead of worrying about the outcome. High achievers know, in measurable terms, what they want to get out of their focused efforts. This type of clarity and focus is empowering.
2. Embrace a growth mindset. The key here is not only the belief in your abilities, but also the belief that you can improve those

abilities with focus, effort, and commitment. We are not seeking perfection, we are interested in pursuing excellence.
3. Manage failure. Failure is inevitable, but if managed correctly, it is a temporary state. Avoid connecting a negative event to a future event. Allow yourself a short window to learn from the setback and move on to the next challenge as an opportunity to succeed and learn.
4. Raise sales-specific confidence. Confidence is an ever-changing state of mind. Identify specific areas of sales fundamentals to create your personal blueprint to create and maintain sales confidence. Committing to the mastery of specific sales skills in your weekly routine will produce optimal results.
5. Protect and nurture your emotional reservoir. This is a critical skill to consistently perform at your best. When we become overwhelmed, our capacity to filter, digest, and prioritize information is compromised, which can lead to bad stress creating a pool of negative emotions reducing our resilience levels.

What Can EdgeThink Provide to Sales Organizations?

- ☐ On-site keynote or kickoff speeches where the most impactful knowledge to your organization is delivered.

- ☐ Training workshops that delve into specific strategies of how to gain a winning edge in sales.

- ☐ One on one sales coaching with your team. All training is tailored both to the organization and the individual – we contradict the one solution fits all strategy.

Now you can gain the winning edge in sales with the attitude of elite athletes - just visit **www.WhatIsYourEdge.com** for more information.

www.ingramcontent.com/pod-product-compliance
Lightning Source LLC
Chambersburg PA
CBHW061228180526
45170CB00003B/1207